W9-BAW-838

THE USBORNE BOOK OF
FACE PAINTING

Chris Caudron and Caro Childs of Lococo

Edited by Cheryl Evans • Designed by Ian McNee
Illustrated by Chris Chaisty • Photographs by Ray Moller

This edition published in 2002 by Usborne Publishing Ltd.,
83-85 Saffron Hill, London, EC1N 8RT, England. www.usborne.com
Copyright © 2002,1993 Usborne Publishing Ltd.
The name Usborne and the devices 🎈 are Trade Marks of Usborne
Publishing Ltd. All rights reserved. No part of this publication may be
reproduced, stored in a retrieval system or transmitted in any form or by
any means, electronic, mechanical, photocopying, recording or otherwise,
without prior permission of the publisher.
First published in America 2003.
Printed in Portugal.
U.E.

Ready to paint

To paint the exciting faces in this book you need water-based face paints. These cost a little more than other kinds, but give much better results. You can buy them from toy shops or theatrical costume suppliers (see page 32). Here's some more about how to start.

Sponges

You can use ordinary make-up sponges, or buy special, thick ones from face paint or theatrical suppliers. It is useful to have two or three sponges to use.

Paint

The paints come in single pots or a palette. They will not harm most skins, but always check for skin allergies first. They wash off with soap and water.

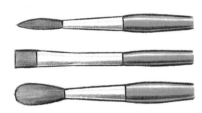

Paint brushes

You need at least one fine brush and one thick one. They may have flat or pointed ends, which make different shapes when you paint with them. Both kinds are useful.

Getting started

Wear old clothes, so it will not matter if you get paint on them (though it does wash off). Make sure your hands and the model's face are clean and dry. Tie back any hair that falls over your model's face. Here you can see the best way to set up to paint faces.

Sit very close to your model, on chairs facing each other.

Have one set of knees outside of the other.

Place paints and water on a table near your painting hand.

Painter puts her free hand on the model's head to keep it steady and turn it from side to side to paint.

Model's hands rest on painter's knees for steadiness.

2

Sponging a base

If it streaks, your sponge is too wet.

1. It is vital to learn how to sponge an even base. Wet a sponge and squeeze hard until no more drops come out. Rub the sponge lightly in circles over the paint.

2. Apply the paint evenly all over the face. Dab and push the sponge onto the face with a twist of the wrist. Don't try to sponge in long, dragging strokes.

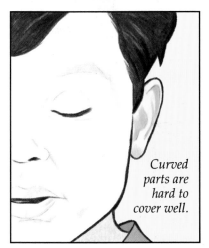

Curved parts are hard to cover well.

Paint right up to hair line.

3. Don't forget the eyelids. Ask the model to look up and work carefully close under his eyes. Dab well into the creases around the nose, mouth and eye corners.

4. Check that the base is neat and even all over. Turn the model's face gently to each side to check the paint on the chin line is not ragged. Correct it if it is.

Brush control

Hold the brush like a pencil, a little above the bristles.

Get it really wet, then wipe and roll the bristles gently across the paint toward you.

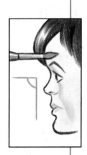

Paint with the brush at a right angle to the face. (The red lines show you this angle).

Lay the bristles flat on the face and press as you paint to make a thick line.

Lift the brush off and paint lightly with the tip to make a fine line or come to a point.

Mouse and rabbit

There are lots of animal faces you can paint. Try to find one that suits your model's face shape and hair. Some animals simply do not work well as their faces are not at all like people's - a horse, elephant or crocodile, for example.

Sugar mouse

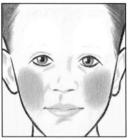

1. Sponge pink onto both cheeks. With white on a brush, paint a curve over each eyebrow. Fill in the shape down to the eye sockets, just below the eyebrows.

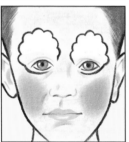

2. Now put black on your brush and do a wavy outline from one corner of the eye to the other, around the white curve. Streak a black line out under each eye.

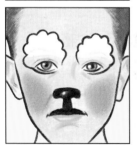

3. Paint the whole end of the nose black. Go between the nostrils, too. Paint a line from under the nose to the top lip black. Then do the top lip black.

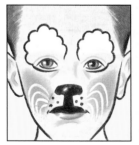

4. Paint black dots on each side of the line from the nose to the top lip. Now with white paint again, do whiskers curving down. Paint the bottom lip bright red.

Tips

Apply with a brush.

You can use pink make-up blusher in place of paint on the cheeks. Face paint suppliers sell other blusher shades.

Face paint is easily licked off lips. For pink or red lips, borrow or buy a lipstick to use. It will stay on longer.

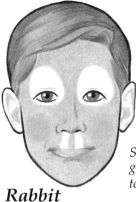
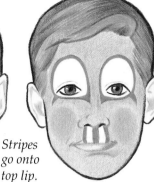

Stripes go onto top lip.

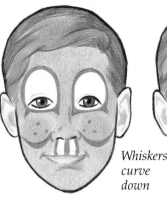
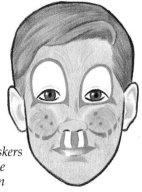

Whiskers curve down

Rabbit

1. Sponge a mauve base and blush pink cheeks. Fill in a white arched shape above each eye and do two white stripes under the nose for teeth.

2. With red, paint smoothly around the white arches. Do a line under each eye that slopes down at both ends. Outline the white teeth.

3. Still with red, paint curves around the rosy cheeks, starting from the bottom corners of the nose. Add three dots on each cheek.

4. With pink, paint the end of the nose and curved whiskers which start from near the red dots. Paint two pink streaks up by each eyebrow.

Finger trick

Here's a way to do smooth brushstrokes. Hold the brush above where you want to start.

Find a place to put your little finger on the face nearby. Paint your line, keeping your finger still.

It may feel strange at first, but it will soon help you to paint confident lines.

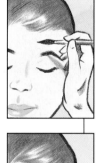

5

Dogs

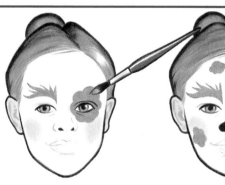

Spotted dog

When you paint a dog, look at your model's face well before you start. Is it round and chubby or long and thin? Try to think what kind of dog it looks like. This one suits a small, round face.

1. Sponge a white base. Add a little pink to each cheek. With a brushful of grey, paint a patch around one eye and a spiky eyebrow over the other eye.

2. Paint a few more small patches on the face, as shown. Now with black, paint the whole end of the nose. Paint a line from under the nose to the top lip.

3. Fill the top lip in with black. Put three black dots on each side of the line under the nose and paint fine, black whiskers out onto each cheek. The ends curve down.

Arrange hair to look like dog's ears.

White streaks next to black whiskers make them stand out more.

4. Do a broad, red tongue over half of the lower lip and onto the chin. Fill in the rest of the lower lip with black and do a streak down the tongue when it's dry.

Technique tip

As a rule, add details from the top down, that is eyebrows first and mouth last. However, once you have paint on your brush, it's a good idea to use it wherever it is needed - do all the black bits you can at once, for example. It may break the rule, but saves rinsing the brush too much.

White-faced dog

For this dog you need brown paint. If you do not have any, you can make it by mixing on your sponge. Rub your sponge in black, then orange and test it on the back of your hand. To make it lighter, rub in some yellow or white.

Brown covers eyes but not mouth.

1. Sponge a broad white stripe down the middle of the face. Then sponge a brown, curved shape down each side, like this. The brown overlaps the white.

2. With black on a brush, paint thick eyebrows and a line under each eye. Paint up the creases on each side of the nose to meet on top and fill in with black.

3. Paint a strip from under the nose to the top lip black. Fill the top lip in with black. Put dots to show where whiskers start on the muzzle on each side of the strip.

Ask your model to try making dog expressions.

Whiskers start near black spots.

4. Paint a red tongue over the bottom lip onto the chin, then do a black bottom lip, as for the patches dog. Do white whiskers curving onto each cheek.

Animal features

Many animals have a split upper lip and whiskers. Features like these help you to recognize them. Think of other typical features to use when you try more animals.

Cats

You can do lots of versions of this cat face. Look at real cats' markings to do pet cats, or look at pictures of the big, wild cats. Use your imagination to create bright fantasy cats.

Always sponge the middle of the cat's face a paler shade than the outside. This makes the face seem to come forward, like an animal's muzzle.

Shading makes these parts sink into face.

1. Sponge a base with a paler middle. Use a contrasting, darker paint to sponge shadows on the forehead and cheeks.

These lines suggest a cat's face.

2. Fill a thick brush with white. Paint whiskery face markings out along the eyebrows. See how to do this in the box below.

3. Paint down the smile lines from nose to lips. Curve up and out to a point on the cheeks. Do it a few times, curving sooner each time.

Eyebrow whiskers

Lay the brush down. Paint a line along the brow bone.

Lift the brush up and off at the end to make a point.

Repeat a few times. Lift the brush sooner each time.

Paint hands to match face, if you like.

Add extra dots and streaks, if you like.

4. Fill in above the top lip with white, except for a strip under the nose. Using dark red, underline the eyes and outline the whiskers.

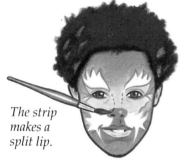

The strip makes a split lip.

5. Paint the end of the nose (under the tip, too), the strip you left below the nose, and the top lip in your contrasting red paint.

6. Put a few red whisker dots on the white patches above the top lip. Finally, paint the bottom lip gold.

Tiger (above)

Give a yellow tiger black stripes and sharp teeth. It is more important to suggest the animal's markings than to be strictly accurate.

Leopard (below)

Sponge a rounded white muzzle and chin on a yellow-brown base. Groups of brown spots suggest a leopard's hide.

Clowns

Traditionally, every clown invents his own face paint to please himself, so no two ever look the same.

Circus clown

The pictures below show you the basic way to paint a clown's face. Look at the big picture and the box on the right for more ideas.

Mouths

Curved up looks happy.

Curved down looks sad.

Paint a big mouth over and outside of the lips. The simplest one to do is a blobby, sausage shape.

Eyebrows

Curved brows

Shaggy brows

Paint eyebrows above the real ones. Happy clowns can have bright eyebrows. Black eyebrows look scarier.

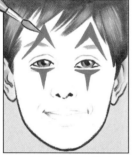

Ask your model to look up as you paint under the eyes.

1. Sponge a white base. Paint thick eyebrows any shape you like. Underline the eyes and do a thin triangle down from the middle of each line.

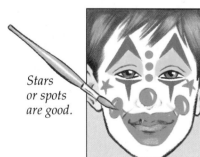

Stars or spots are good.

2. Paint a red nose and a big mouth. This one goes out onto the cheeks and ends in big red dots. If you like, add more bright shapes.

This clown has thick, pointed eyebrows.

His eyelids are painted up to the eyebrows, with spots on.

Leave a streak of white in cheek dots to make them "shine".

Pierrot

Pierrot (say pee-air-oh) clowns are beautiful, but often sad. Take time to do a thorough, even, white base first. Then the few strong details show up well.

The black hairband and painted point on the forehead suggest a Pierrot's black skull cap.

This mouth is painted narrow, with higher points and a more curved bottom lip than her real lips.

Leave a streak of white on the tear for "shine".

Tip

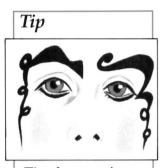

This face works best if the two sides are not quite the same: paint different eyebrow shapes in step 2.

1. Carefully sponge a white base. Sponge or blush the cheeks lightly, with pale mauve or blue.

2. Load a brush with black paint to do fancy eyebrows. Curl them down onto the cheeks.

3. Paint a fine black line out under each eye. Outline a big teardrop shape under one eye only.

4. Paint the eyelids in a delicate shade up to the line of the eye socket. Do a gold tear and pink lips.

11

Witch and vampire

These eerie faces are good for witches, space aliens or supernatural creatures. Work on a really subtle base first, then add the details.

Changing shape

These effects look best on mean, lean faces. You can make any face look thinner by clever shading. Here's how you can do it.

1. Start with a creepy base such as white, green or mauve. Shading should be darker so sponge it with a little black, dark mauve or deep blue.

2. Shade the eye sockets. This makes the eyes seem to sink deeper.

3. Stroke the sponge down both sides of the nose so it looks bony.

4. Make the cheeks hollow by darkening under the cheekbones.

5. Shade the side edges of the chin.

Witch

Fluorescent green looks unearthly.

1. Sponge and shade a bony green face, as shown on the left. It would work just as well using blues or mauves.

Exaggerate eyebrow shape.

2. Pick a strong contrast for brushwork. Press and paint a line out along each brow bone. Lift the brush up at the end to make a point.

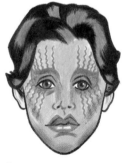

Join underline to brows, if you like.

Use a thin brush for spiky lines.

3. Sweep a line out under the eyes for emphasis. Paint spiky, wavy lines up from the eyebrows and down from the eye underline.

Make points of top lips higher.

4. Paint the lips in your contrast shade. Tell your model to keep her mouth gently closed. Exaggerate the top lips and fill them in.

Vampire

Extend black down sides of nose.

1. Sponge a thorough white base. Shade it in grey (see left). With black on a brush, do wicked, shaggy eyebrows and underline the eyes.

Outline outside of lips.

2. With black, outline the lips and paint sharp fangs down from the corners of the top lip. When they dry, touch up the fangs with more white.

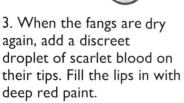

You can sponge black onto fair hair, if you like. It washes out.

3. When the fangs are dry again, add a discreet droplet of scarlet blood on their tips. Fill the lips in with deep red paint.

Hag

To paint an evil old hag, sponge a pale base with dark shading. Then ask your model to screw up her face. See where creases appear and paint along them with fine grey and brown lines. Do lots of small lines off the main ones and add some white lines for highlight. Do shaggy grey eyebrows and thin lines across the lips.

Stipple (page 23) sideburns, if you like.

Brush hair back and paint a black "widow's peak" on forehead.

Skull and ghoul

These are faces to frighten your friends or wear to a scary party. There are more party ideas on pages 30-31.

Skull

1. Sponge a white base. With a very dry sponge, dab just a little green around the edges, to look like mold.

Ask model to close his eyes while you paint his eyelids.

2. Sponge grey shadows under the cheekbones. Load a brush with black and paint a circle around each eye.

Triangles end around tops of nostrils.

3. Paint two long, black triangles on the end of the nose for the holes where the skull's nose used to be.

Cover hair with black material or a hood to get the total skull effect.

Touch up "teeth" with more white.

4. Outline a big, black oblong around the mouth. Paint black lines across it, leaving white, lumpy "teeth".

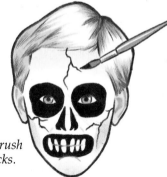

Use a fine brush for thin cracks.

5. Paint jagged, forked cracks in black. If you paint white lines beside them they look as if they are really deep.

Ghoul

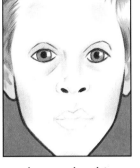

Cover the mouth with white so that it disappears.

1. Sponge a thorough white base. Shade the temples, sides of the nose, cheek hollows and chin in grey.

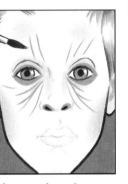

Add thin streaks across eyebrows, too.

2. With pink on a brush, circle the eyes and around the nostrils. Do several thin pink streaks under the eyes.

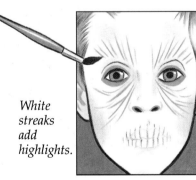

White streaks add highlights.

3. Paint thin, grey wobbly lines across the eyebrows and mouth. Add thin grey lines under the eyes, too.

Skeleton

You can place a whole skeleton on a face, like this. Put a skull on the forehead. Do the arms over the eyebrows. Put the spine and ribs down the nose and the pelvis around the nostrils. Legs go down the creases between nose and mouth. Do the shapes in white, and outline finely in black.

Wrap head and body in a white sheet for the ghostly look.

Monsters

Purple, yellow and dark blue are all good for monster faces. You can see how to do scales and horns here to make them even more frightening.

Scaly reptile

1. For a reptile, sponge yellow from forehead to mouth in a rough "U". Sponge the rest of the face green, blending where they meet.

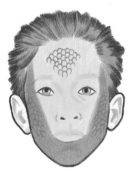

2. With dark green or black on a thin brush, paint scales like overlapping curved shapes in a triangle up the forehead and cheeks.

3. Do big black ovals around the eyes and over the eyebrows. Do nostrils as for the skull (page 14). Paint a black oblong around the top lip.

4. Paint white fangs down from the corners of the lips. With gold paint, put a forked tongue over the lower lip and onto the chin.

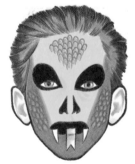

5. When it is dry, fill in the rest of the lower lip with black. Add a dash of dark green or gold inside each of the scales, if you like.

Horns

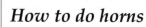

Horns slope gently out from inner top corner of eye patches.

Dots of red on fangs and in eye-corners make a striking contrast.

How to do horns

Load a brush with white.

Lay the brush, slanting, onto the face. Press down, twist and lift off.

Do the same again, above and a bit to one side of the last one.

Repeat until the horns are long enough. Make the last stroke more upright.

When the strokes are dry, paint dark red, sloping lines between them.

1. Sponge shades of mauve for a two-tone base. Put the darker shade on the forehead, under the cheekbones and around the chin to make hollows.

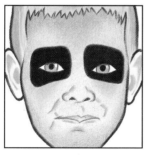

2. Blush the forehead, cheeks and sides of the chin with pink. With black on a brush, paint big, roughly square eye patches.

3. Paint a black, downturned clown's mouth (see page 10) with a thick brush. Do black nose-holes as for the skull (see page 14).

4. When the mouth is completely dry, add white fangs up and down from the corners of the lips. Then add the horns as shown above.

17

Butterflies

How you place a butterfly on a face is very important. Paint the outlines carefully, as shown here, then use your imagination to paint them as brightly as you like. Here are some ideas.

Tip

Both sides of a butterfly should match as nearly as possible. If you do the side you find harder first, it is easier to make the second side match. For right-handed people the left side is usually harder, and the right side is harder if you are left-handed.

1. With blue on a fine brush, sweep a sloping line up the forehead from the top of the nose. Stop about level with the middle of the eye.

2. Now curve down beside the eye, then underneath it back to where you first started. Ask the model to look up and go close under her eye.

3. Starting in the same place, paint another line that curves around the cheek, about down to the level of the bottom of the ear.

You can do step 3 in two ways: go down beside the nose then around the cheek, or out under the eye first and up by the nose. Try both ways.

Correcting mistakes

If the shapes don't match, change both until they do (shown by red dotted lines). You can only do it by making them bigger.

To be sure the wings match you must add the "wrong" lines to each, too. They look messy, but will blend in when you paint over them.

More butterflies to try

After step 4, try these other ways to finish the butterfly: just add the body; add the loops and body; do loops, scallops and body. Or just do the outline, loops and scallops on a pretty base.

The butterfly above is done on a pale yellow base with blushed cheeks. The wings are mainly blue to match the model's T-shirt. The scallops are done lightly in black so that they show up nicely.

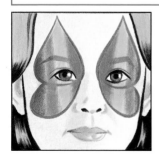

4. Do the other side of the face to match (see above if you go wrong). Fill the shapes in brightly. Paint from the nose out to the edges.

5. With a thin brush and white paint, make a long, smooth loop around each eyebrow. Do another loop in the middle of each bottom wing.

6. With white, make small loops around the big ones. Try not to lift your brush off the face. Then do a scalloped edge all around the wings.

7. Streak a long, red body down the nose (it must join onto the wings at the top). Add a round head, feelers and contrasting stripes.

19

Garlands

These garlands look nicest draped across the forehead and down beside the eyes, curling onto the cheeks. The steps on the right show you the basic way to paint a garland. In the box below you can see how to do some flowers and leaves to put on it.

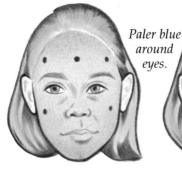

Paler blue around eyes.

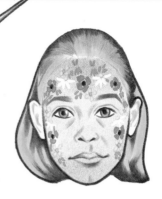

1. Sponge a two-tone blue base. Add pink to the forehead, cheeks and chin. Place dots where you want to put the middles of your biggest flowers.

2. Add the big flowers' petals. Now scatter small dots in between, where you will put smaller flowers. Then add their petals, too.

3. It's best to end with a small flower on each cheek. Leaves can link flowers and fill in gaps. Join them with thin, green stems, if you like.

Daisy

Side view

Do a yellow dot. Load a pointed brush with white. Lay it down, pointing at the dot, then lift up for each petal.

Primrose

Do a small orange cross. For double yellow petals, press a brush down, lift up, then press again, a little to one side and over lapping.

Winter wreath

Sponge a pale green base. Shade pink on the forehead, cheeks and chin. Paint a garland of leaves (see below), instead of flowers.

Holly

Paint a gold curve. Add green looping points around it, meeting in a point at each end. Fill in with green. Add red berries with a white dash for "shine".

Mistletoe

Paint two long, oval pale green leaves on a stem. Do two pale yellow berries and add tiny dots to them. Do a dark stripe down the leaves if you like.

Ivy

Tendrils

Paint a green leaf shape with three points, like this. Do gold lines from the middle out toward each point. Add a few curling tendrils.

Anemone

Do a large black dot. For petals, get red on a thick brush, lay it down beside the dot and move it around a bit to make a blob.

Rose

With a thin brush, paint a pink or red spiral. Lay the brush down and move it around to make three open petals around the edge.

Violet

Do a small yellow dot. Lay down a brush lightly for petals. Do two above and three below (press harder for bigger petals).

Leaves

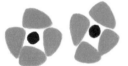

Lay a brush with green on it down gently. Do leaves in pairs, with one at the end. Their shape depends on the brush (see page 2).

Ribbons

Red ribbons and bows make this a special Christmas wreath. You could loop red streaks through the wreath and add bows, as shown below, on each cheek.

Do a blob with a loop on each side.

Two ends wiggle down from the blob.

21

Sunset scene

The secret of this face is to blend paint in several strata (bands) across the face. Then add a few simple shapes to suggest your scene. Silhouettes can be very effective. These are outline shapes completely filled in so you recognize what they are by their shape, not by details on them. You can see some silhouettes on the faces shown here.

1. Sponge the whole bottom of the face turquoise from the chin up over the top lip and about level with the bottom of the ears.

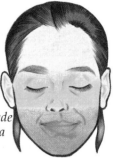

Dab to blend the strata together.

You get another shade where strata blend.

2. Working quickly, so the turquoise is still damp, blend yellow on a sponge up over the nose and cheeks and across the eyelids.

Shade cheeks, chin and forehead.

3. Sponge pink over the eyebrows and purple on the forehead. Stripes tend to flatten a face. Give it some shape with purple shading.

Branches curve with the shape of the face.

4. Load a medium brush with black and paint four palm branches. The box on the page opposite shows you how to do them

Palm branches

Start with the tip of the brush, press and make a thick curve, then lift off to make a point.

From the same spot, curve a branch over each brow, one down the nose and one up the forehead.

Add fine, spiky curves from underneath each main curve to make palm fronds (leaves).

Paint branches over nose and forehead.

Black lines for silhouettes of grass on chin.

Do gold lips and crescent moon.

Orange squares look like lit windows in the church.

Snow scene

Blend white, yellow then shades of dark blue up the face. Dab purple on cheeks and forehead. Paint a bare tree and church in black.

Add white for snow on the branches and the church. Do snowflakes with a stipple sponge (see below) or the point of a fine brush.

Stipple sponge

A stipple sponge is made of coarse mesh. You wet it, squeeze it, then rub it in paint and dab gently on the face to make speckles. It's good for snowflakes, stars, a stubbly chin, or a hazy, romantic look on any face. You can buy a stipple sponge from face paint or theatrical suppliers.

Add an island for tree to stand on.

5. Do a line of black blobs with spaces between for the trunk. Each time, press the brush down, then lift. Make them curve onto the cheek.

White wavy lines suggest waves.

Do white ripples around fin.

6. Add more silhouettes, as you like. A curved black triangle on the chin makes a shark's fin; V-shapes in the sky are birds; or try a ship.

Don't overcrowd the face with details.

7. Streak gold on the joints of the trunk as if they are being caught by the sunlight. Make the face glow with a round gold sun and gold lips.

23

Designer patterns

You can paint striking faces using shapes and patterns on things you see around you. Look at natural things, such as tree trunks or leaves. Or notice what is behind your model, such as a wallpaper design, and camouflage the face to blend in with it. One idea is to make a face to match her clothes. See how parts of the T-shirt pattern have been used below.

1. Look closely at your model's clothes. Pick out a pattern, or part of one, that you like. Then mix your paints to match.

2. To mix, dab a sponge in one pot, then another and test on the back of your hand; or mix brushfuls of paint on a saucer.

Dots, black wavy lines and orange flower match T-shirt.

A design like this is a good idea if your model does not know what kind of face she would like painted.

This pattern has a plain white base.

3. Choose a light base shade from the pattern and sponge it on. Do a more interesting two-tone base (paler around the eyes) if you like.

Underline eyes in black so they show up well.

4. Now add the pattern. You do not need to copy exactly, just pick out the strongest or nicest parts. See the opposite page for how to place them.

Placing a pattern

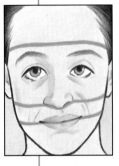

To fit a pattern to a face, place strong lines across on eyebrows, mouth or under the nose.

Put strong vertical lines down the nose or down through the eyes.

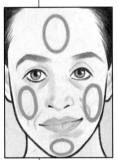

Place main features of the pattern where there is lots of space: on the forehead, cheeks and chin.

Matching

You do not need to copy a pattern to make a face co-ordinate with someone's clothes. Simply paint any of the faces in this book, using shades that go with what they are wearing.

Match-a-bike

This face has been painted to match a green and black racing bike. You can adapt it to match any sports gear.

Sponge two main shades diagonally across the face. With a stipple sponge (page 23), speckle each shade with dots of the other along the join. Add a motif, or symbol. Paint the lips to contrast.

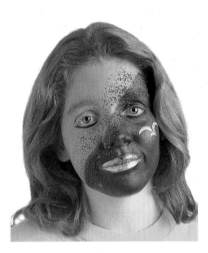

Football crazy

A design like this can show you support a sports' team.

Sponge opposite quarters of the face white. Sponge the other quarters to match the team's gear. When the white is dry, add stripes to match the other quarters with a brush. Straight lines are hard to paint, so do them slowly and carefully.

Graffiti

Writing on a face is fairly tricky. Words with an uneven number of letters work best since you can put the central letter in the middle of the face then add the rest on either side (take great care with spelling - it may help to write the word down on paper first). The best places to write are across the nose or forehead.

Robot

Silver and gold paint do not show up very well by themselves on most skins. If you mix them with green, blue or mauve, though, they make a shiny, metallic effect which is great for robots, monsters or aliens.

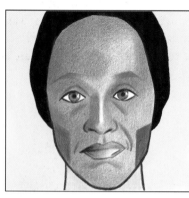

1. Mix deep blue with silver and sponge a base. With dark blue on its own, sponge straight-edged shadows from cheekbones to chin.

You could paint gold dots on corners of eye patches.

The dots look like rivets, which are what hold metal sheets together.

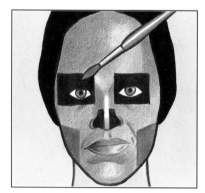

2. With a brush, paint big, black squares around the eyes and fill them in. Do thin black rectangles on the nose above the nostrils.

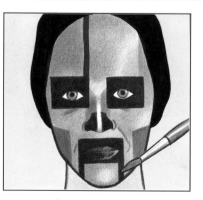

3. Paint a black oblong around the mouth. Do some thin, straight lines on the face, to look like where metal sheets are joined.

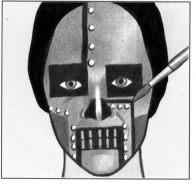

4. Place small white dots along the lines. Outline half of each dot in black. Add thin gold lines across the mouth, like a grille.

Kabuki

In Japan there is a long tradition of face painting. Kabuki is an ancient form of Japanese drama in which the actors, who are all men, paint their faces in bold, mask-like designs to represent characters. For this Kabuki lion, first sponge a thorough white base.

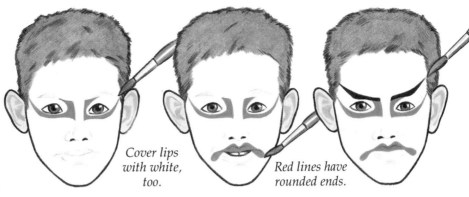

Cover lips with white, too.

Red lines have rounded ends.

1. Paint thick red lines from the inner eyebrows, down the sides of the nose. Then paint out under the eyes and curve up and off to a point.

2. Paint the top lip red and extend each side down onto the chin. Ask the model to keep his lips apart until dry, so the red does not smudge.

3. Do thick, black eyebrows. Press on your brush and sweep out along the brow. Lift off and curve up to a point at the outer edge.

Red, white, black

The Kabuki face above uses only red, white and black paint. Here are some more you can try.

Always do a thorough white base first, then add the red details, then the black ones.

There are lots of other faces in this book you can do using only red, white and black (mix them to make pink and grey, too): see mouse (page 4), spotted dog (page 6), vampire (page 13), skull (page 14), and ghoul (page 15), for example.

Sponge red on hair, if you like.

Owl

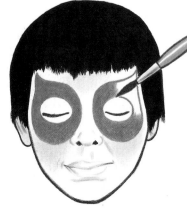

The beak joins up the eye shapes.

Paint dot on lid over where eyeball is.

Keep eyes closed until dry.

1. With brown on a brush, paint an owl's face shape around the eyes. Fill it in except for a circle on the lid and just under the eye.

2. Paint a yellow triangle for a beak on the nose. Put orange in the circles you left unpainted on the eyelids and under the eyes.

3. When the brown is dry, do white streaks out all around the eyes. With black, outline the orange circles and put a dot in each.

You can do the owl face on a base. You don't need to sponge around the eyes, but cover the nose well.

Cover the lips with base. All attention should be on the eyes.

Add black streak down middle of beak.

When the model closes his eyes, the owl opens his.

4. Outline the whole shape in black to tidy up the edges. When the black eye spot is very dry, add a white blob for a gleam of light.

Bat

Join back up to where you started.

Paint from middle to edge of shape.

1. Sponge a yellow base. With black on a brush, slant a line up the forehead from the top of the nose to make a big point above the eye.

2. Do looping points down the side of the face and two long points down to about mouth level. Curve back up to the top of the nose.

3. Do the other side to match. Outline a circle around the eye sockets and just under the eyes. Fill the rest in with black.

Do the outline on the side you find hardest first (see page 18).

Add gold eyes and streaks across body.

Two or three lines fork from same place.

Do gold details on the black, when it is very dry.

Paint lips black to complete the face.

4. Do a head and long body down the nose. Underline the eyes in gold. Make gold veins fork out from near the eyes to each point.

29

Party pieces

You can use your face painting skills to have fun at parties. You and your friends could paint your best faces on each other, or try doing faces all on the same subject to make a theme: you could do a tiger (page 9), some clowns (pages 10-11) and the strongman, lion and seal from these two pages for a circus theme, for example. You could take photographs to keep as a record.

Here are some more faces to inspire you. Some are variations on ideas from earlier in the book and some are for special occasions.

Pumpkin

Do an orange base. Paint red curved stripes down the face that meet at the chin. Do black triangles over the eyes and on the end of the nose, and a black zig-zag mouth to make a carved pumpkin.

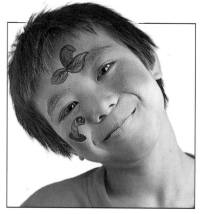

Apple

Do a halloween apple with a green base and pink cheeks; put leaves and a stem on the forehead. Paint half a worm on the cheek, with a black circle across the end to look like a hole in the apple.

Strongman

Do a white base and blush pink cheeks; add thick, black curly eyebrows and a line under each eye; paint a black, twirly moustache and red lips. He could also be the circus ringmaster.

Lion

Do a cat face (see pages 8-9) with a yellow-brown base and white, sponged muzzle. Lions have a beard so sponge the chin white, too. Try to make the hair stick out like a lion's mane if you can.

Seal

Do a seal with a white base and mauve shading. Add grey eye patches and a muzzle. It has black whiskers, nose and lips. Can the model make a seal noise and slap his arms together like flippers?

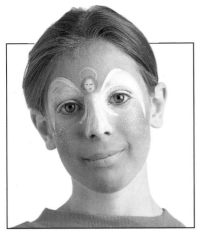

Angel

Sponge a sky blue base and blush the cheeks. Stipple (page 23) white stars. Paint wings across the eyebrows, a robe down the nose, and arms on the cheeks. Add a head and halo.

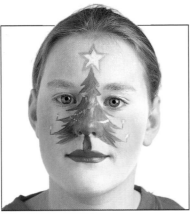

Christmas tree

Sponge a white base. Paint a green fir tree down the nose. The branches spread onto the cheeks. Do a brown trunk from the nose to top lip and add decorations as you like. Paint red lips.

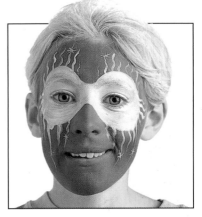

Iceman

Sponge a mid-blue base, leaving a mask shape around the eyes. When the blue is dry, paint the mask shape white. Do thin, white icicles all around the edge of the mask. Add white stars.

Japanese doll

On a white base, sponge a pink band from brows to nose tip. Do a white line down the nose. Outline the eyes in black, making a point at the side. Slope black brows up. Do a small, red mouth.

Valentine

Paint a special garland (see page 20) for Valentine's or Mothers'Day. Do a white base and pink cheeks; add hearts and ribbons. Can you think what to do for a Fathers'Day face?

Grey rabbit

Here's another version of the rabbit on page 5, with a grey base instead of purple. You could do the same face on everyone at a party, but paint each one to match the person's clothes.

Portrait gallery

Here are photographs of all the children who had their faces painted for this book. At the bottom of this page it tells you which pages you can see them on. Have a look at the photographs, then see how different some of them look in their face paint; or try to guess which faces they modelled before you look at the list.

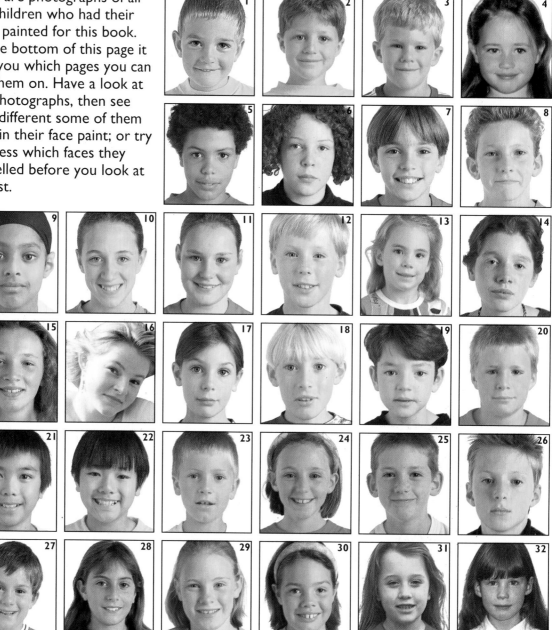

1. Henry Swallow: p17. 2. Jonny Greensted: tiger p9. 3. Sam Greensted: p7. 4. Amelia McKilveney: p6. 5. Lucy Palmer: leopard p9. 6. Rupert Palmer: p8. 7. Christopher Sweeney: vampire p13. 8. William White: p16. 9. Sukhbir Rihal: skeleton p15. 10. Alice Skidmore: p24,26. 11. Lydia Childs: p21,22, Christmas tree p30. 12. Alastair Baird: p14. 13. Aimée Baird: p18. 14. Caroline Radway: p12, bike p25, lion p30. 15. Mary Caudron: p19, Valentine p31. 16. Daisy Caudron: p23. 17. Stefanie Fuller: hag p13, angel p30. 18. Damion Fuller: iceman p31. 19. Oliver Pugh: p29, seal p31. 20. Sam Jenkins: graffiti p25, strongman p30. 21. John Lau: p28, apple p31. 22. Chun Lau: pumpkin p31. 23. Alex Jones: football p25. 24. Rachel Mylon: Japanese doll p30. 25. Wesley West: p15. 26. Damian Phillips: p27. 27. Oliver Wiffen: p10. 28. Jemima Bokaie: p11. 29. Kate Lewis: p20. 30. Karen Divall: rabbit p31. 31. Francesca Tyler: p4. 32. Hannah Kirby-Jones p5.

To find face paint suppliers, look in your yellow pages telephone directory under **Fancy dress**. Ring and ask if they supply water-based face paint. Some makes to ask for are Grimas (U.K.), Mehron's and Stein's (U.S.A.).